The Horrible Hands

Mick Gowar

Illustrated by David Roberts

Chapter 1
The Haunted Fens

This is a story about the Fens in years gone by. The Fens are the flat lands in the East of England. The Fens are cold, and the Fens are wet. Sometimes, cold East winds blow across the Fens. It's so cold that the water freezes in the ditches and rivers. Then the Fen people get out their skates and race each other all the way from Ely to Cambridge.

But sometimes the winds blow so hard that the trees bend right over. Windows rattle and the wind moans down the chimneys like a poor, lost ghost. That's when the Fen people gather round the fire and tell each other scary stories.

They tell stories about ghosts who haunt the fen roads. And stories about bogles, nasty little goblins who steal milk from the cows in the fields. Or steal bread from the pantries in the farm kitchens – even when the kitchen doors are locked and bolted.

But the scariest tales they tell (on the nights when the East wind wails down the chimneys) are about the horrible hands. Hands without arms. Hands without bodies. Hands that crawl out of the ditches and rivers on cold, dark nights. Hands that'll crawl right up your trouser-leg and pinch the money out of your pockets. Or, if you've no money, they'll pinch your handkerchief.

Or, if you've no handkerchief, they'll crawl up your trouser-leg – Owww! – pinch your bottom, and scuttle away!

I've never seen one of these horrible hands. But there are lots of Fen people who say they have. I don't know whether they really believe the stories of the horrible hands. But I do know that, even today, the old Fen men and old Fen women won't go out after dark without a keepsafe in their pockets.

Don't you know what a keepsafe is? Then I'll tell you. It's a charm. A special thing with magic powers, that'll keep you safe. Safe from ghosts, safe from goblins, and safe from the horrible hands.

A hundred years ago, everybody who lived in the Fens had a keepsafe. Some people carried a lucky penny in their pockets. Rich folk bought medals with a picture of St Christopher on them, to keep on a silver chain around their necks. And poor folk had a rabbit's foot tied to a bit of string around their necks.

No. That's not quite true. Not everybody had a keepsafe. Not everybody believed in ghosts and goblins and horrible hands. Long Jem Hawkins didn't believe in any of that – and look what happened to him! Don't you know what happened to Long Jem? Then I'll tell you.

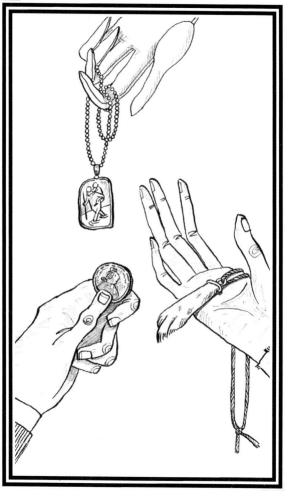

Chapter 2
The Tallest Boy in Grunty Fen

Jem Hawkins was the tallest boy in the village of Grunty Fen. By the time he was eleven years old, he was nearly six feet tall. At twelve, he was nearly seven feet tall.

"He must have Viking blood in him," said Mr Fyle, the village schoolmaster, who knew all about history.

"He must have giraffe blood in him," said Tom Carter, who didn't know about anything.

"Nonsense!" said Jem's mother, who was only five feet tall. "It's the pickled beetroot sandwiches I always give him for his lunch."

Whatever the reason was, Jem was the tallest boy anyone in Grunty Fen had ever seen. And the villagers called him Long Jem, because he was so tall.

Now, a hundred years ago you could leave school when you were twelve – if you could find someone who would give you a job.

Jem was so tall and strong that Farmer Taylor gave him a job as soon as he was twelve. None of the other lads in Jem's class got a job – they were all too small and puny for farm work.

So while the other lads were learning their sums and spellings, Jem worked on Farmer Taylor's farm. He picked the stones out of the fields before ploughing. He waved his heavy, wooden rattle and hollered to scare the crows away from the seeds. He picked the last ripe apples from the top branches of the trees that no one else could reach.

Long Jem was very proud of his job on the farm. He was too proud. Every morning, when he was on his way to work, Jem would pass the other lads on their way to school. He'd point at them and shout, "Look at you babies – off to school! I'm doing a proper job and getting good money. Too bad you're so weak and weedy!" Then he'd stick out his tongue.

This made the other lads in the village very cross. "Just because he's half-giraffe, doesn't mean he can pull faces at us and call us names!" said Tom Carter.

"He's no better than us," said Davy Pike. "So why should he get a job, while we have to stay at school?"

"It's just not fair," said Peter Penny, and the other two lads agreed. And even though Jem was twice their size, Tom Carter, Davy Pike and Peter Penny began shouting rude names back at Jem whenever they saw him.

"Oi! Long Jem Hawkins! Spider legs!"

"Hey! Long Jem! What's the weather like up there?"

"Hi! Long Jem! You've got crows nesting in your hair."

Then they would sing a silly song:
"Long Jem! Tall as a tree!
Arms like bean poles, brain like a pea!"
"You load of babies!" Jem shouted back.
"Go and learn your spellings and your sums. A working man like me hasn't got time to chat with little boys like you!"

That made the boys even crosser. So they decided to get their own back on Long Jem.

The next Sunday, after church, the three lads waited beside Farmer Taylor's barn.

"Oi, Long Jem!" shouted Tom, as Jem walked past. "What do you call a boy with horse dung all over his Sunday clothes?"

"I don't know," said Jem. "What do you call a boy with horse dung all over his Sunday clothes?"

"Jem Hawkins!" shouted all the lads together, and pelted Jem with horse dung.

That made Jem really angry, so he chased the three lads right across Farmer Taylor's big field. He caught hold of Tom just at the edge of the wood on the far side of the field.

Jem grabbed Tom and lifted him high up into a beech tree so the collar of his jacket caught around a high branch. Then Jem walked away, leaving Tom dangling from the branch, shouting and wailing.

16

Tom's parents begged and begged Jem to lift their son down. But Jem just stood there with his hands in his pockets, scowling and shaking his head. In the end, the Ely Fire Brigade had to be called to get Tom down.

After that, the lads stop calling Jem rude names, but they were plotting revenge.

It was about this time that Old Jacob saw the horrible hands crawling across Fen Road.

Chapter 3
The Horrible Hands

It happened one night at the end of
November. It was a cold evening. Fog had
come down across Grunty Fen. The fog
was thick and yellowy-green, like leek
soup. Old Jacob the farmhand had been
ploughing, but he'd decided to stop for the
day when he couldn't see the far end of
the field.

"I was just leading old Dobbin out of the field to go back along Fen Road when I saw them," he told the villagers later.

"Three of them creeping out of the ditch. They were white and bony, and they glowed as they crept across the road. It was horrible! There were no arms and no bodies, just three horrible hands glowing in the fog!"

Everyone who lived in Grunty Fen believed Old Jacob's story. Everyone, that is, except Long Jem.

He just laughed when he heard Old Jacob tell the story of the horrible hands.

"You must be soft in the head if you believe in all that nonsense," said Jem. "Horrible hands – pah! It was the fog, and your poor eyesight. That's why you saw white hands crawling out of the ditch. Put your spectacles on, Jacob. Then you won't see nasty things on your way home!"

And he laughed even harder when the lads clutched their keepsafes as Old Jacob told his story.

"What's the matter? Big babies! Clutching your charms! What are you – men, or frightened old ladies?"

The lads glared at Jem. They hated the things he was saying, but they kept a tight grip on their keepsafes all the same.

Tom Carter had a St Christopher medal his grandmother had given him for his tenth birthday. He always wore it round his neck.

Davy Pike always wore a little copper bracelet that his mother had bought from a gypsy fortune-teller at Stourbridge Fair.

And Peter Penny had an old, worn rabbit's foot that he always kept in his trouser pocket. If he was out on the dark fen roads at night, Peter would stroke his rabbit's foot and mutter:

"Hare of the Fen! Hare of the Fen!

Keep me safe, till I'm home again ..."
all the way home.

Of course, Long Jem had no keepsafe.

On dark winter nights, Tom, Davy and Peter nervously touched their keepsafes as they walked home from school. But Jem would stand at the side of the road and jeer at them as they walked past.

"Look at those babies," he'd call out, to anyone who would listen. "Scared of their own shadows! Davy Pike's so frightened that his wrist has gone green! Tom Carter's wetter than an old sponge. And just look at Peter Penny with his rabbit's foot! Look at the bunny boy!"

And Jem would laugh and laugh.

Tom, Davy and Peter got so fed up with Jem laughing at them that they decided to get their own back.

"I've got a plan," said Tom, one evening when the three lads were in the school room, after lessons had finished.

"I've thought of a way to scare Long Jem so badly that he'll never scoff or sneer at us again."

"Oh, yes – what's your plan?" asked Davy.

"Next Saturday, it's the Christmas dance at Farmer Taylor's barn. Long Jem will be there – so will the whole village. We'll give Long Jem Hawkins the fright of his life!" said Tom. "And we'll make a fool of him in front of the whole village."

"How are we going to do that?" asked Peter.

"You two wait here, and I'll show you," said Tom.

He picked up a white cloth bundle from underneath his desk and went outside.

Two minutes went past. Three minutes.

Then suddenly the classroom door burst open. There in the doorway stood a terrible figure. It was covered in a white sheet and its face glowed white.

"Aaaargh!" yelled Davy. "It's a ghost!"

Peter dived under his desk and pulled out his rabbit's foot. "Don't let it get me! Don't let it get me!" he cried.

The ghost roared with laughter. "Don't be daft!" it said. "It's only me – Tom."

Davy and Peter stared at the terrifying figure.

"Tom – is it really you?" asked Peter.

"How did you do that?" asked Davy.

"Simple!" said Tom. "Just an old bed sheet, and some chalk on my face. And if it frightened you – well, think how frightened Long Jem Hawkins will be when *three* horrible ghosts jump out from behind the barn and grab him!"

"He'll scream his head off!" said Peter.

"He'll go running home to his mother, howling like a baby!" said Davy.

"We'll scare him so badly he won't be able to walk across his own kitchen without a keepsafe!" said Tom.

Chapter 4
The Christmas Dance

On Saturday night, the three lads put on their best clothes, and off they went to the Christmas dance in Farmer Taylor's barn.

Outside the barn, the wind was moaning. There was the smell of snow in the air. But inside the barn it was warm and light.

Then at about ten o'clock, one of the younger children – who'd been playing outside – came rushing in through the door shouting, "It's snowing! It's snowing!"

All the children rushed to the door and watched the thick, white flakes swirling in the wind. But the grown-ups weren't so pleased. They moaned and complained.

"Time to go home," they all agreed. "Before it gets any worse!"

Out of the barn danced the children, laughing and happy. Out of the barn stomped the grown-ups, muttering and puffing.

Tom, Davy and Peter looked at each other and nodded. It was time for them to go, too.

As usual, Jem sneered and scoffed and laughed at them as they got up to leave, clutching their keepsafes.

"You're just like a flock of frightened chickens," laughed Jem.

Before the three lads could reply, there was a call from the far end of the barn.

"Hey! Long Jem!" shouted Old Jacob. "Can you get these lanterns down? They're too high. I can't reach them."

As Jem went to help Old Jacob, the lads hurried out of the door and round the side of the barn. They crouched down in the shelter of the wall, where the shadows were thickest. They each pulled an old bed sheet out from underneath the old horse trough, where they'd hidden them earlier. They quickly wrapped themselves in the sheets.

Then they whitened their faces with three sticks of chalk which Tom had 'borrowed' from school.

In just a few minutes, they looked like three terrifying ghosts who'd come to haunt the disbelieving Jem.

"Long Jem won't laugh when he sees us," said Tom, as the three lads crouched down in the shadows.

"You're right," said Davy. "This will be one lesson Long Jem Hawkins will never forget!"

Chapter 5
Horror in the Snow

Inside the barn, Jem handed the last lantern to Old Jacob.

"I'll keep this one alight," said Old Jacob. "It'll help us find our way home. Just the candles on the tree to blow out, then we're finished."

Jem started blowing out the candles on the Christmas tree. One ... two ... three ... As he blew each candle out, the barn got darker and darker. Soon, the only light was coming from the lantern that Old Jacob was holding.

Whoooah! Whoooah! went the wind, blowing through the cracks in the walls of the barn.

Screeak! Screeak! went the hinges of the big barn doors.

"You're looking a bit nervous, Jem,"
said Old Jacob. "Not afraid of going out
there are you?"

"Me?" said Jem. "Me? Of course not.
I've told you. I don't believe in all those
stories of ghosts and goblins, and hands
crawling out of the Fens."

"Well, I'm all right," said Old Jacob. "I've got my keepsafe with me. Have you got yours, Long Jem?"

Jem shook his head. "I don't need a keepsafe," he said. But now he didn't sound so sure.

A sudden noise of something high up in the darkness made Jem jump.

Tip! Tap! Tip! Tap!

"What's that noise?" asked Jem.

"Probably just a bat up in the roof," said Old Jacob. "What did you think it was, Jem – one of the horrible hands trying to get in?"

"Ha-ha-ha …" Jem tried to laugh. "Of course not!"

Tip! Tap! Tip! Tap! came the sound again, but louder this time.

"Let's get home," said Old Jacob. "I don't like this weather."

As they crouched by the barn, Tom, Davy and Peter were beginning to have second thoughts about the surprise they'd planned for Jem.

The wind was blowing harder than ever. Big flakes of snow were landing on their heads, and then melting and running down the backs of their necks. The melting snow on their faces made the chalk dust on their faces run down their cheeks like milky tears.

Suddenly there was a rustling sound, like something small scampering quickly along the road.

"What's that?" asked Davy.

"Quickly! Get into your places," whispered Tom. "I think Jem's coming now."

They crouched down beside the old stone horse trough and waited for Jem to appear out of the darkness.

"Where is he?" muttered Peter.

"I don't know," said Tom. He peered over the top of the horse trough. Then Tom felt something pulling at his sheet.

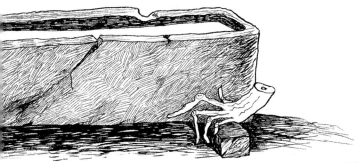

"Hey! Stop that!" he whispered. "Stop tugging at my sheet, Davy!"

"No, you stop tugging at mine!" hissed Davy, from the other end of the trough.

"I'm not tugging at your sheet," said Tom.

"Nor am I tugging at yours," said Davy.

For a moment, the tugging stopped. Tom looked down, and what he saw made the hairs on the back of his neck stand up on end. It was a hand. But it couldn't be Davy's – it didn't have an arm or a body. A white, bony hand, like a ghostly crab, was tugging at his sheet.

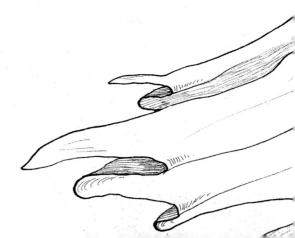

"It's pulling at my sheet!" yelled Tom.

"It's pulling at mine, too!" shouted Davy.

"Aaaaargh – the horrible hands!" they both screamed.

"Come on!" shouted Peter. "Let's get out of here."

Inside the barn, Jem heard the screams.

"What was that?" said Jem.

"I didn't hear anything," replied Old Jacob. "Mind you, my ears aren't as sharp as they once were. Come on lad – it's time to go home."

Jem opened the barn door. He felt a tapping on the toe of his boot. He looked down – and gasped. It was one of the horrible hands. Then he felt a tap on the other foot. There was another! Then he felt something crawling over his ankle. A third one! Three horrible hands!

Before Jem could move, one hand ran up his leg, over his chest and pinched him on the nose.

"**Oww!**"

Another hand climbed up his leg, over his chest, onto his shoulder and pinched his ear.

"*Oooooh!*"

The third hand clambered up the back of his leg, and pinched his bottom.

"*Aaaargh!*"

Before Old Jacob could help or stop him, Jem was off across the field, with the three horrible hands hanging on to him.

"**Oww!** *Oooooh*! *Aaaargh*! Get them off me!" shouted Jem, as he disappeared into the darkness.

A few moments later, there was a loud splash – as if someone had either jumped or fallen into Farmer Taylor's duck pond.

It wasn't until long after midnight that a bedraggled Jem Hawkins limped home.

He was wet through and frozen to the bone. And he was covered from head to foot in green slime and thick, black mud from Farmer Taylor's pond.

Chapter 6
Keepsafes for Jem

Jem had to stay in bed for a week to get over his terrible experience.

A couple of days after the dance, Tom, Davy and Peter came to visit Jem. He told them the story of the horrible hands. How they'd grabbed him by the ear, the nose and the bottom. And he told them how he'd had to jump into Farmer Taylor's duck pond to make them let go.

The next day, Old Jacob came to visit Jem. He heard the story, too. Soon, everyone in Grunty Fen knew about Long Jem and the horrible hands. The story even got onto the front page of the *Ely Chronicle*.

After that, Tom, Davy and Peter stopped trying to scare Long Jem – they didn't need to. And Long Jem didn't tease them about their keepsafes any more.

After that terrible night, Jem wouldn't go anywhere near Farmer Taylor's barn ... unless he had a St Christopher medal round his neck, a copper bracelet on his wrist and a rabbit's foot in his trouser pocket!